AF614925

ANIMALS AT RISK!
California Condors
by Rachel Grack
BLASTOFF! 2 READERS
BELLWETHER MEDIA • MINNEAPOLIS, MN

Blastoff! Readers are carefully developed by literacy experts to build reading stamina and move students toward fluency by combining standards-based content with developmentally appropriate text.

Level 1 provides the most support through repetition of high-frequency words, light text, predictable sentence patterns, and strong visual support.

Level 2 offers early readers a bit more challenge through varied sentences, increased text load, and text-supportive special features.

Level 3 advances early-fluent readers toward fluency through increased text load, less reliance on photos, advancing concepts, longer sentences, and more complex special features.

★ **Blastoff! Universe**

Reading Level

Grade K

Grades 1–3

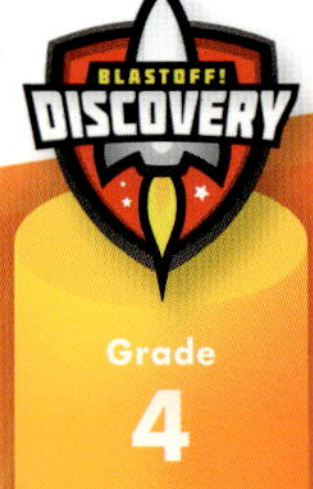

Grade 4

This edition first published in 2024 by Bellwether Media, Inc.

Library of Congress Cataloging-in-Publication Data

LC record for California Condors available at: https://lccn.loc.gov/2023036157

Editor: Kieran Downs Designer: Brittany McIntosh

Printed in the United States of America, North Mankato, MN.

Table of Contents

Giants of the Sky

California condors are the largest birds in North America.

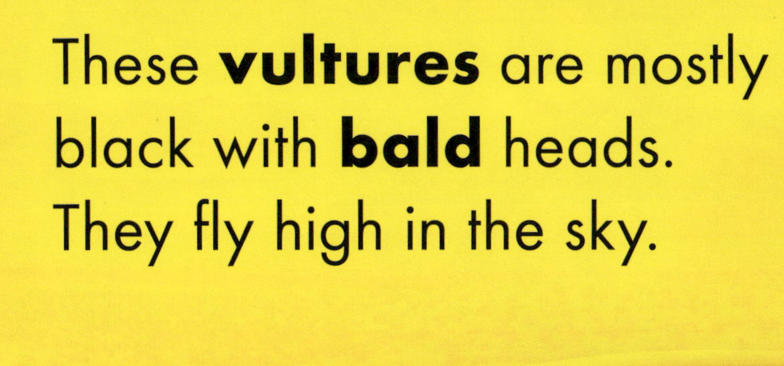

These **vultures** are mostly black with **bald** heads. They fly high in the sky.

California condors once lived across North America. But people caused deadly problems.

The birds almost died out. Today, they are **critically endangered**.
California Condor Range
N
W
E
S
range =

In Danger!

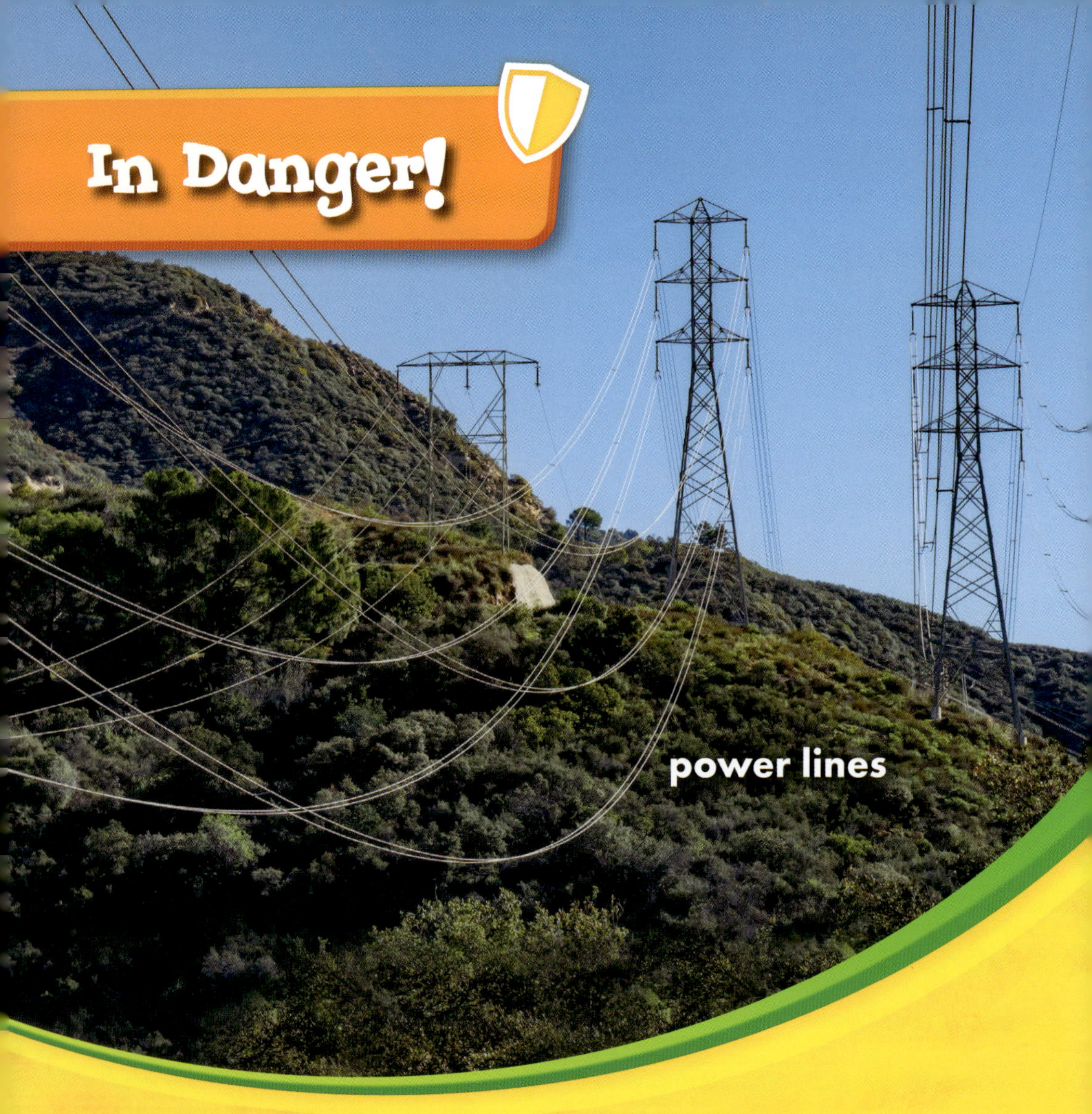

California condors need wide-open **home ranges**. But people spread into these lands.

The birds may fly into power lines. They also get hit by cars.

Threats

1 people need roads and cities

2 power lines go up

3 California condor homes are less safe

California condors are **scavengers**. They may eat **carrion** left by hunters.

But some hunters use **lead bullets**. The lead gets into the meat. Birds that eat it get sick.

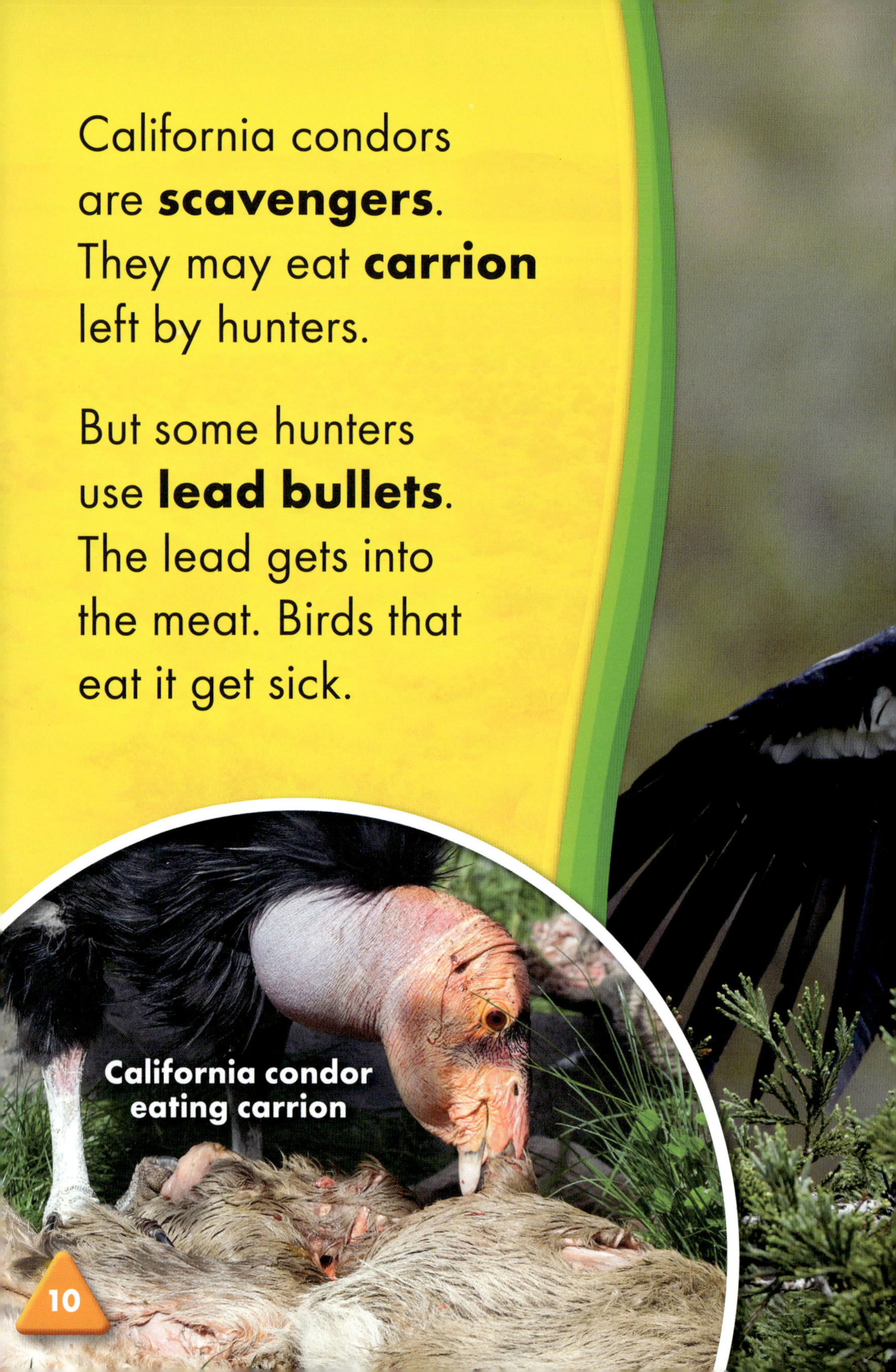

California condor eating carrion

California Condor Stats

Least Concern	Near Threatened	Vulnerable	Endangered	Critically Endangered	Extinct in the Wild	Extinct

conservation status: critically endangered

life span: around 60 years

Save the California Condors!

California condors are important to their **ecosystems**.

They clean up dead animals. This keeps their homes healthy. It also helps plants grow.

The World with California Condors

People have been working to save California condors for years.

Hunters may choose non-lead bullets. Governments can also ban lead for hunting.

California condor in a zoo

Wildlife workers raise California condors in zoos. The birds stay safe.

Healthy birds are set free into the wild. Their numbers are slowly growing.

Governments set aside land for California condors. They keep people away from nesting spots.

California condor nesting spot

The birds have larger homes.
They have space to fly freely.

Donations help wildlife workers care for California condors. Some people teach others about the birds.

Everyone can find ways to save California condors!

Glossary

bald—without feathers

carrion—the remains of a dead animal

critically endangered—greatly in danger of dying out

donations—gifts for a certain cause; most donations are money.

ecosystems—communities of plants and animals living in certain places

home ranges—the lands on which animals live and travel

lead bullets—objects fired out of guns made from a harmful metal called lead

scavengers—animals that eat dead animals for food

vultures—large birds that eat dead animals

To Learn More

AT THE LIBRARY

Gleisner, Jenna Lee. *Condors.* Minneapolis, Minn.: Jump!, 2020.

Riggs, Kate. *Vultures.* Mankato, Minn.: The Creative Company, 2023.

Sabelko, Rebecca. *California Condors.* Minneapolis, Minn.: Bellwether Media, 2019.

ON THE WEB

FACTSURFER

Factsurfer.com gives you a safe, fun way to find more information.

1. Go to www.factsurfer.com.
2. Enter "California condors" into the search box and click 🔍.
3. Select your book cover to see a list of related content.

Index

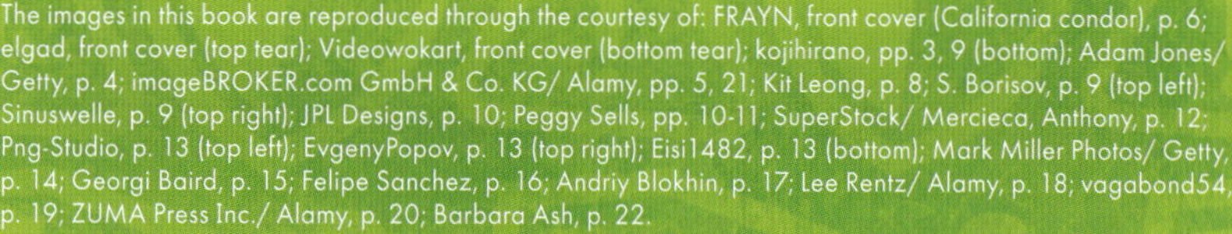

The images in this book are reproduced through the courtesy of: FRAYN, front cover (California condor), p. 6; elgad, front cover (top tear); Videowokart, front cover (bottom tear); kojihirano, pp. 3, 9 (bottom); Adam Jones/ Getty, p. 4; imageBROKER.com GmbH & Co. KG/ Alamy, pp. 5, 21; Kit Leong, p. 8; S. Borisov, p. 9 (top left); Sinuswelle, p. 9 (top right); JPL Designs, p. 10; Peggy Sells, pp. 10-11; SuperStock/ Mercieca, Anthony, p. 12; Png-Studio, p. 13 (top left); EvgenyPopov, p. 13 (top right); Eisi1482, p. 13 (bottom); Mark Miller Photos/ Getty, p. 14; Georgi Baird, p. 15; Felipe Sanchez, p. 16; Andriy Blokhin, p. 17; Lee Rentz/ Alamy, p. 18; vagabond54, p. 19; ZUMA Press Inc./ Alamy, p. 20; Barbara Ash, p. 22.